Time to Make It
STOP

The beauty of the
soul is constant,
continuous and
endless.

Time to Make It

STOP

The HOW of Now

Written and
Illustrated by **Jim George**

To Peggy, my *present*, and to all the clients who made this book possible.

Foreword

Now. Right now. When's the last time you were there? When was the last time you weren't busy remembering the past or mentally projecting yourself into the future? Oops. Sorry. By simply answering that question you had to pop right back out of the present moment and into the "past".

See how tricky and elusive this "Now" thing is? For most of us, our minds are filled with so much past/future noise and clutter that we don't even notice it anymore. It seems normal. It's what we do. We seem stuck in time, haunted by past events and either anxious about or eager to get to something we call "the future". If you think about it (and just doing so pretty much guarantees that) we spend surprisingly little or no time "here" in the present. That's a shame because there is some pretty real magic right here in this gift, this *present* we call Now.

As the title suggests, this book is less about the "what" or "why" and more about the "how" of Now. Over the centuries, much has been written about the present moment, *about* Now. Mystics, sages, gurus, spiritual teachers and even physicists have described a rarified, altered and almost mythic state called *the present* and yet, for most of us, that state remains just as vague and illusive as ever.

Thinking about Now, *talking* about Now is not *experiencing* Now. It's more like being in the attic above a party. Something wonderful is going on "there" and yet *you* are still "here" separated from it.

The personal discovery of *being* this state and the increasing ability to return to it any time, any place, for any reason has been the single most important gift I've ever been given. This gift has changed everything in my life.

I believe that this gift is the fundamental birthright of each and every one of us and that it is ours for the taking if and when we are ready to let go of our past and future illusions and realize that this state – this *being* – is in fact who and what we *are*.

The goal of this book is for you to begin to *experience* Now, first in little glimpses, then gradually more and more until you fully realize that Now is all there *is*, ever *has been* or ever *will be*. To that end, I'm using as many different kinds of communication as I can to help break the patterns that keep us locked in the old ways of seeing ourselves and the world in which we live.

There is a sense of lightness and joy in the Now. I hope you will begin to feel it as you explore this book. I will not be telling you anything you don't already know at some level. If some of what you see, hear or read here resonates with you it is because some part of you already knows it and just needed to be reminded. Welcome to the book. Welcome to the Now. Welcome home.

Jim George
March 28, 2011

So, here you are. "Now".

How are things? Are you happy? Content?
Are you feeling anxious or worried?
Angry? Sad?

Are things going well?   Not so well?

How do you *know?*

The answer to that question may be the first step to unlocking more joy, more fulfillment, more *success* than you ever dreamed possible.

In order to answer the question, I'd like to introduce you to someone you may think you already know. You might even think it's you. It's *not* you.

I'd like you to meet:

your *mind...*

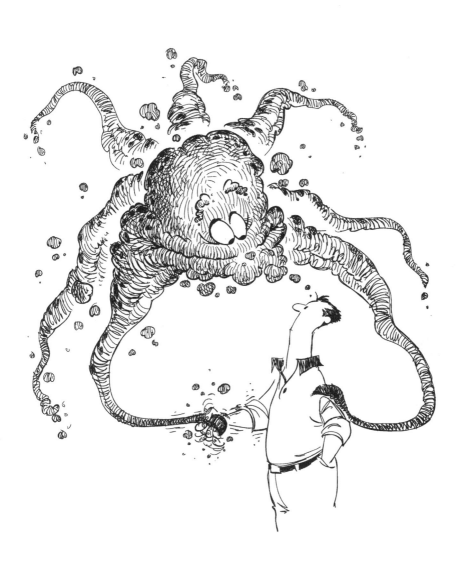

Your mind is really, *really* busy...

It has lots of things to do.

It has to keep track of all the stuff that
makes up your past.

(That's right, I did say
            makes up your past...)

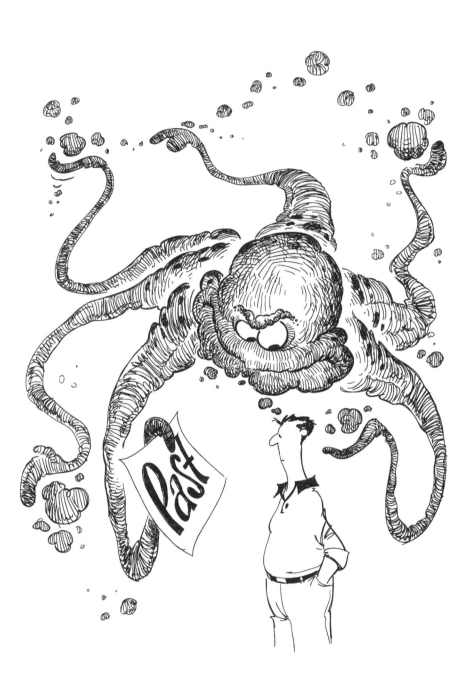

... stuff like Mom and Dad...

... your third grade teacher,
that gym coach...

... your first date...

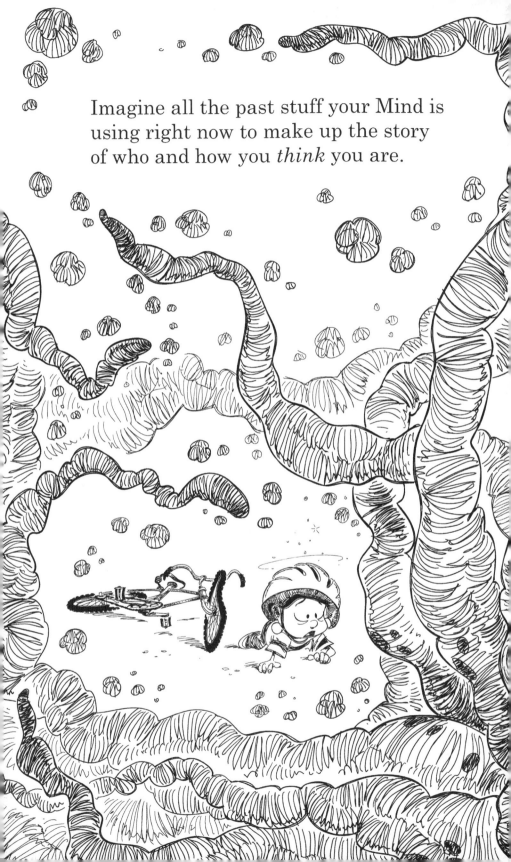

Imagine all the past stuff your Mind is using right now to make up the story of who and how you *think* you are.

It does it so much and so well you
hardly even know it's there...

... and it's not just *you,* either. Pretty much **everyone** is walking around most of the time in a "mind fog" of stuff from the past, a "past" that only exists in their mind...

... a past that limits who and what they are *now*.

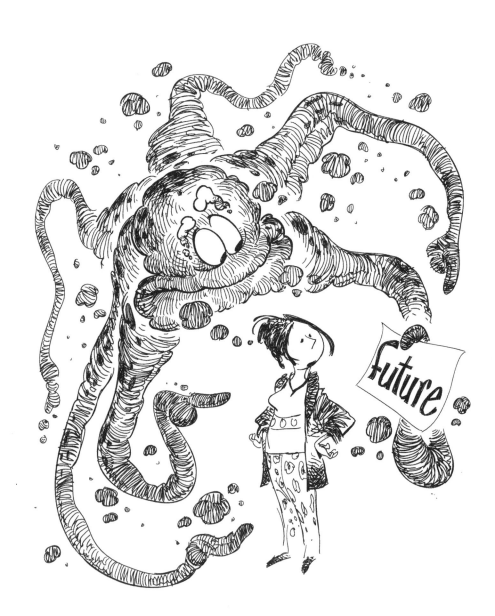

As sobering as that may be, it's only *half* of the story. As if our minds don't have enough to do, they're busy making up "the future" as well...

... a whole world of "What-ifs" and "If-onlys"...

... that only exist in our mind.

There's nothing "wrong" with this. In fact, it's one of the crowning achievements of human evolution. This past-and-future-creating mind is the greatest *tool* in history. Without it, there would be no art, no literature, no great cities, no inventions, no religion, no science – none of the things that make us, well...

... human.

It just happens to come at a
terrible cost.

If we're not very, *very* careful, that past-and-future-creating tool can run away with us. It can even convince us that we *are* that tool – that past and future – and nothing could be farther from the truth.

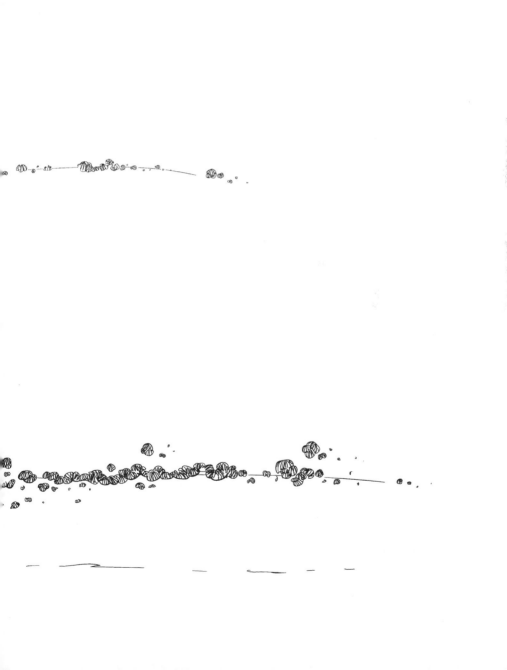

That's where "you" step in. The *real* you. The *being* part of "human being" that exists underneath and beyond the layers of mind-fog "past" and "future".

The *being* that is more than just your body *or* your mind…

That real you – that *being* – is conscious
and aware and because it is a being, like
all beings, it exists *now*... not "then".

Being is what happens *now,* not in
 "back when" or "what if".

Being is what you *are,* not what you
 "were" or "might be".

It's almost impossible to conceive of this while you still believe that you are your mind and your thoughts. However, even your busy mind can't keep the truth from popping up every now and then...

Have you ever had the experience of becoming "lost" in some activity?

It could be as passive and quiet as watching a sunset or as demanding and active as skiing down a challenging slope but, for that magic moment, you found yourself completely focused, present and, perhaps strangely, "at one" with what you were doing.

You weren't "thinking" about anything. You just "were" and time seemed to just... *stop... or expand... or what?... cease to matter or even exist?*

Ever wonder why people become obsessed with such seemingly diverse activities as extreme sports, yoga, racing, fighting, meditation, sex or even military combat?

If experienced to their fullest, each of these activities has one thing in common: each requires and perhaps *elicits* a state of complete and utter *presence*. Each brings the full participant into "Now".

It's not uncommon to hear people say that they have never felt more alive than when they were "lost" in such activities. Some even describe it as *ecstatic*.

Yet, the feeling always seems to fade
the moment they "come back" to the
"reality" of their day-to-day life...

... a "reality" that may not be all that *real*
at all.

What's remarkable about the mind and the past and future that it is constantly creating is just how *real* this past and future *seems* to be.

Because it is made up of the same
sensory information that we take
in all the time, we can actually "see",
"hear" and "feel" the past and future
our minds are creating as if it's *real*.

We perceive it as though it's
        actually *happening*.

This can trigger any number of powerful and primal emotions, often setting off a series of automatic survival patterns in the body known as the "fight/flight" response.

When we're "triggered", our survival instincts take over and we instantly go into a kind of perceptual tunnel. This *tunnel vision* keeps us narrowly focused on immediate survival.

It prevents us from taking in any
information that doesn't support
this sudden urgent need to
either fight or get away.

That response is exactly what we need if we're being *physically threatened.* It has served us well and allowed us to survive for thousands of years.

However, that response was only intended
to last for a few seconds, minutes at most.

Once the immediate threat was removed, our triggered tunnel vision would return to normal perception once again.

But what if the "threat" isn't what's happening *now* at all? What if the "threat" is being created and replayed constantly by the mind as past and future events, triggering a recurring survival state in which the body is constantly torn between the instinct to fight and the desperate need to escape?

What if *this* is the new "normal"?

In this new normal, perceived "threats" don't need to be just *physical* in nature to trigger the fight/flight response. They can be *psychological* or *emotional* as well. Nor do they need to be blatant or explicit. They can be subtle and implied.

The mind can infer a threat to your survival in your boss's tone or your partner's glance. A simple message from a friend can send you right into a tunnel with most of your resources blocked and unavailable just when you may need them the most.

Even with minor triggers, your body still thinks it's being attacked. Faster than the speed of thought, fear-based emotions take over. These emotions are fueled by powerful stress hormones, concentrated chemicals pumping into your body to prepare it to fight or run for its life. It can feel as though you're on drugs...

... because you *ARE* on drugs!

Sound familiar?...

For most of us, there is only one way to come back out of a fight/flight survival tunnel. Whether it's a major crisis or a minor irritation, it takes *time* to return to "normal" – to "come back to ourselves".

A moment or two, an hour, perhaps over-
night, a stress-free amount of time called
a "refractory period" is required for the
body to "down-regulate" from survival
mode back to "normal" mode.

But in today's "new" normal, the mind continues to replay past and future images over and over again. The body becomes triggered, *re-triggered* and re-triggered *again*.

Our thoughts become threats and they
follow us wherever we go, whatever
we do. We spend more and more of our
time in past/future tunnels with half
of our brain and most of our resources
tied behind our backs.

This nightmare roller coaster ride simply *has* to stop...

But... *how?*

The answer lies in a
        perfectly named *gift* called...

... the *Present.*

There is another simple way to bring yourself right out of a fight/flight "survival tunnel" any place, any time, *every* time.

This tool will allow you to regain the intelligence, the clarity, the inspiration and the creative problem solving capacity that is lost *by design* when we are triggered and in high-stress "survival mode".

By bringing your full attention to the present moment, with no perception of "past" or "future" – not even a *split-second* ago or from "Now" – you break the cycle of trigger and response, of "threat" and fight/flight. In fact, when you are utterly in the present, with no perception whatsoever of past or future, it is neurologically impossible for you to even *have* a negative emotion.

Hard to believe? *Try* it...

Try being angry or sad or guilty with no perception of the "past" – not even a split-second "ago"…

What's there to be angry or sad or guilty *about?* Where would it have to be *in time?*

Try being afraid, anxious or worried with no perception of the "future" – not even a split-second from "Now"...

Notice where you have to go in time in order to feel afraid, anxious or worried. Those emotions have no meaning without some degree of future perception.

By focusing all of your attention like a laser beam on the single point in time and space called "Now", you interrupt the process of being triggered. You break the "past/future" pattern long enough to emerge from your perceptual tunnel a completely different "you" than you were just moments ago.

You are no longer limited by the state of mind and body that is the fight/flight response. You are no longer intoxicated by mind and body-altering drugs that so narrow your perception as to render you temporarily stupid, insane or both.

I promised that this was a book about the "How" of Now rather than the "What" or "Why" of Now.

That means it's time to enter some potentially new territory. It'll be fun, I promise. Ready?...

In order to learn how to use this gift, this present called "Now", it's important to remember that...

... *you* are not *your thoughts.*

If you are *thinking* about
what's happening...

... then you are at least one thought
removed from what's happening.

Thinking about what's happening is like being in the attic above a party...

There's nothing wrong with that as long as you remember that it's not the same as *being* at the party.

Thinking about things automatically shifts your attention from "Now" and places it either in the "Past" or in the "Future".

By simply _thinking_, you are focusing your awareness at least one thought away from "Now".

Again...

... nothing "wrong" with that but
it's important to remember that's
what's happening.

Then, of course, one thought leads to another until before long you wind up like a crazed hound dog chasing rabbits into the woods. There's no telling *where* you'll wind up.

One thing is certain, though:
Wherever it is, it *won't* be "Now".

So here's the first piece of potentially new territory. The way to come back to the present moment is not to *think* about it but, rather, to do the exact *opposite:*

The secret to returning to "Now" is to momentarily *stop thinking altogether.*

Of course your *mind*
may have ***other*** ideas...

... or should I say other *thoughts?*

It's not only *possible*, it is **essential** to stop the noise and the chaos in your mind every so often. Learning to do so will change everything in your life forever. It just might *save* your life as well.

But what is it like to *stop thinking* for a moment? More importantly, what is it like to do so *by choice?*

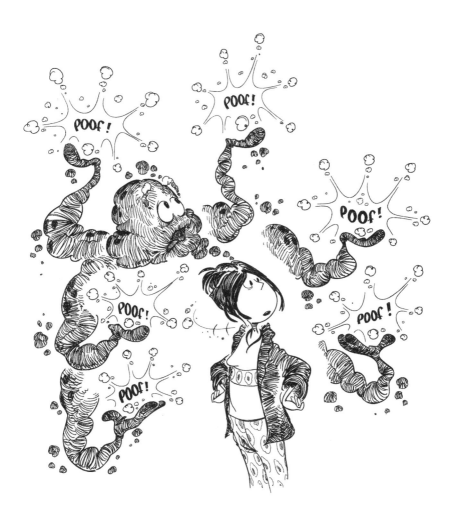

Let's start by using your body's own signal that everything is going to be just fine: **BREATHE!** Give yourself permission to do it *consciously*, right now. Give it a try.

I don't mean those shallow little half-breaths you've been taking this whole time; I'm talking about a nice *slow, deep, FULL* breath... all the way in.

Hold it at the top...
and just let it go nice and slowly.

Ahhhhh...

Now, before your mind can jump in there with more noise and chatter, just focus on what you're doing as you take an even *deeper* breath... *all* the way in... even deeper... and hold it at the top.

Now, slowly just *let it go* as if you are letting go of all stress, all tension, all thoughts of daily life.

With each breath, just notice the tendency for things to begin to slow down, even just a bit, and become more calm, more relaxed, more *still* the deeper you allow yourself to breathe.

As you continue to breathe...

... allow yourself to focus...

... on each word that you read...

... as... you... slowly... read... *each... word...*

... one... word... at... a... time...

imagine... letting... each... word... go... now...

... just ... drifting ... slowly ... effortlessly ... into

...y allowing yourself to just notice the difference as the words return...

... and your mind resumes its "normal"
activity of creating the "Past" and "Future".

You may notice that it's a little quieter and more peaceful there in your head than it was a moment ago.

If so, good. If not, that's alright.

We're just feeling what it's like to stop the noise and the chatter without creating more of it by *thinking* about it.

Before your mind has a chance to start chasing those "thought-rabbits" again, give yourself permission to take another *deep* breath.

Remember, that's your body's signal that *everything is going to be just fine.*

As you slowly release that breath, notice
how it becomes a little easier to just
be here for the moment.

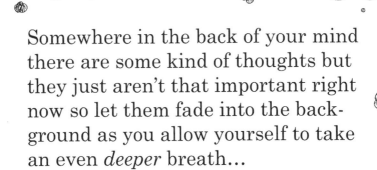

Somewhere in the back of your mind there are some kind of thoughts but they just aren't that important right now so let them fade into the background as you allow yourself to take an even *deeper* breath...

... *all* the way in... and *slowly* release
it along with any remaining tension
or thoughts of any kind.

Ahhhhhhhh...

Now, without asking how or why
begin to focus your attention on
the very center of who you really are.

So quiet, so still... something in you
knows where that is. *Trust* it. You
don't have to *think* about it just *do* it.
Just focus your attention on where
you know the core of your true self is
as you breathe deeply
            into that place, *now*...

... and with a single act of will, as you *exhale quickly*, silently say to yourself the word...

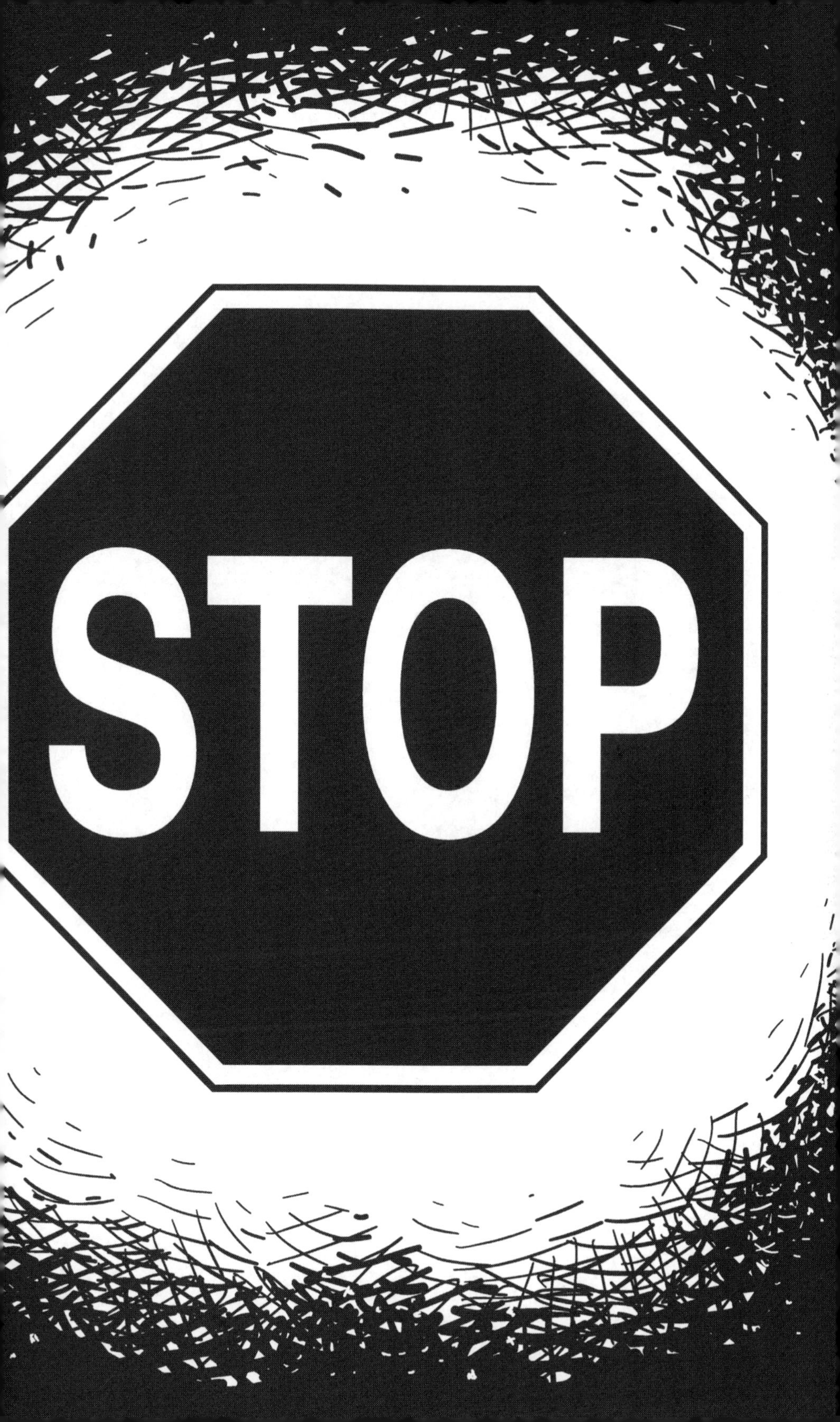
STOP

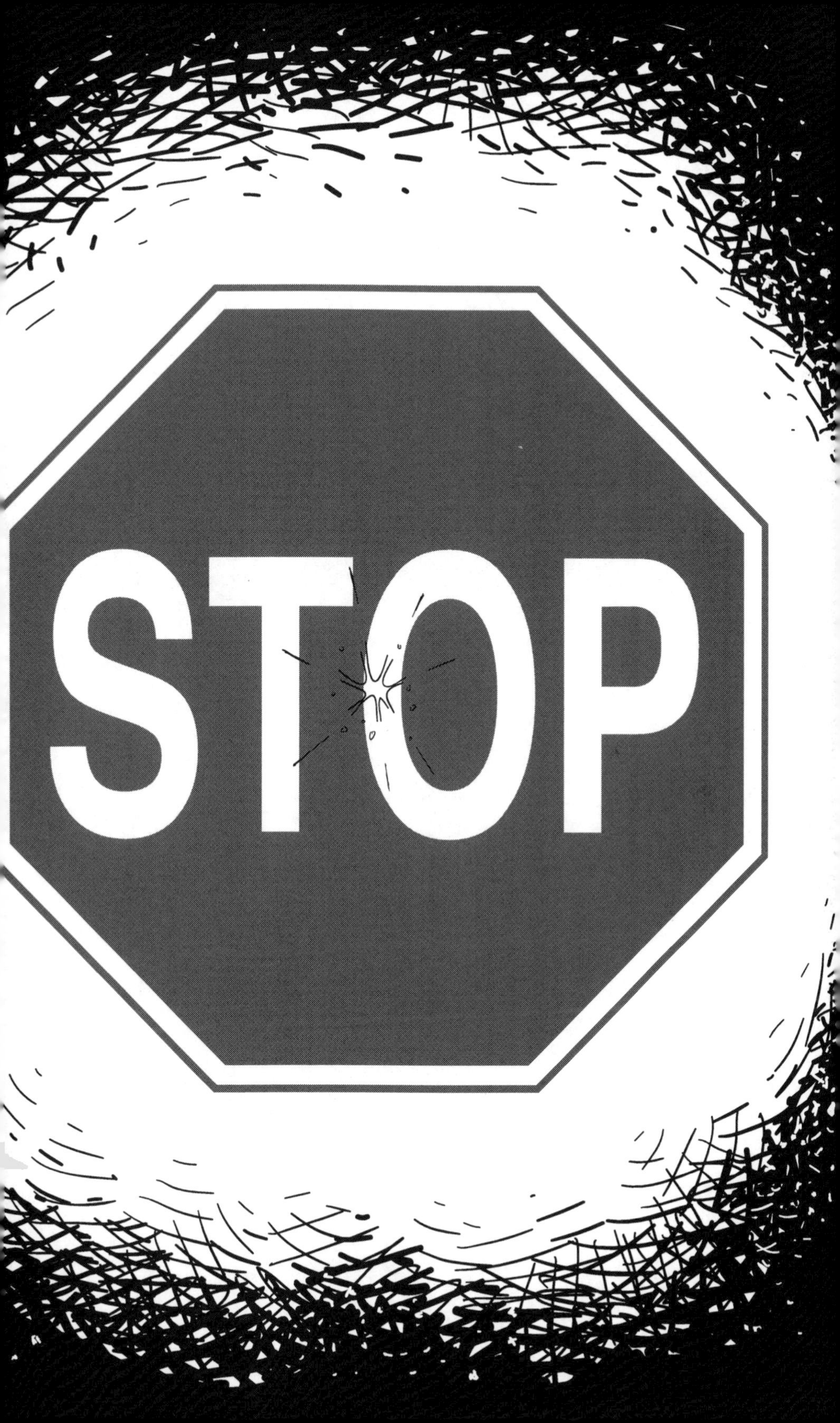
STOP

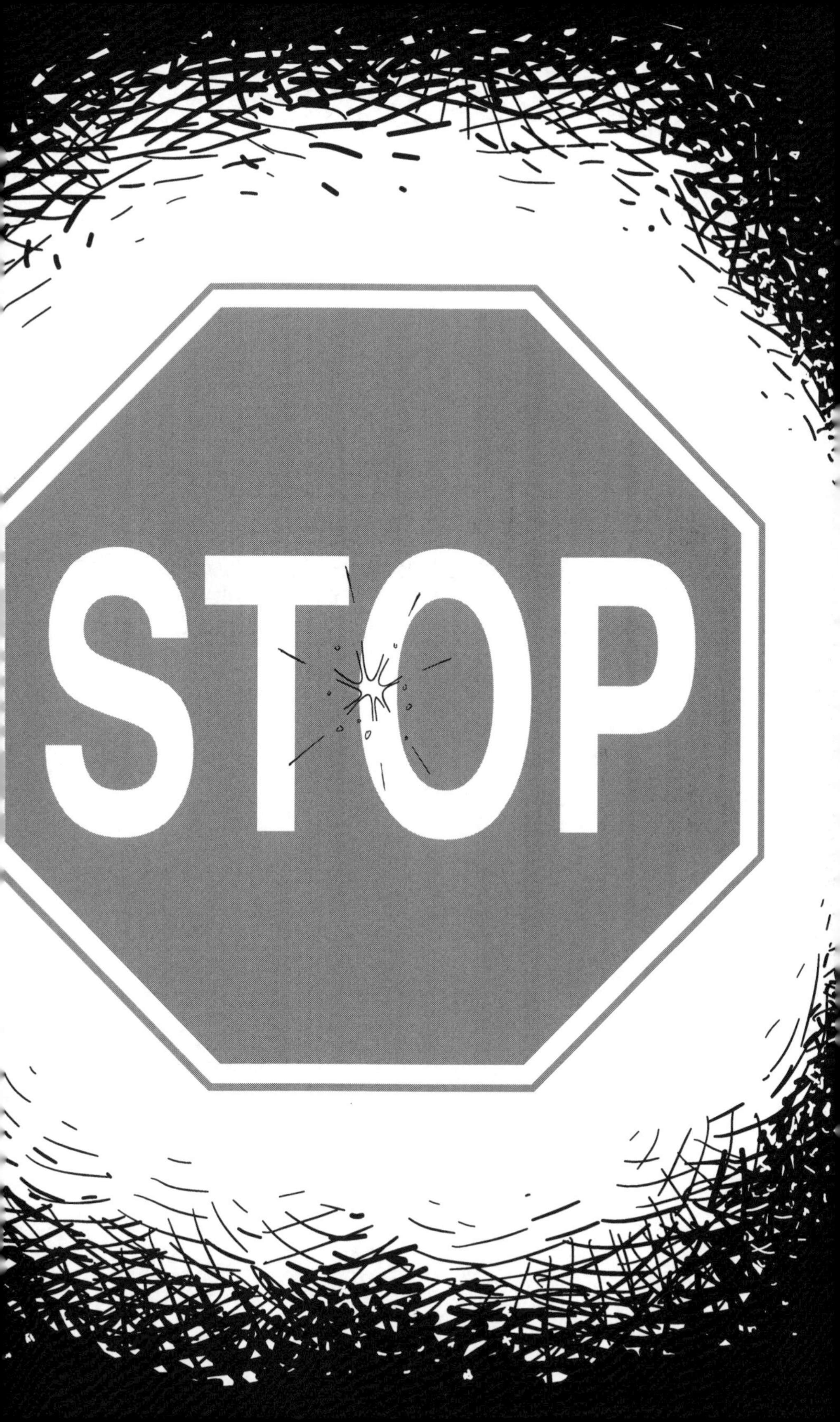
STOP

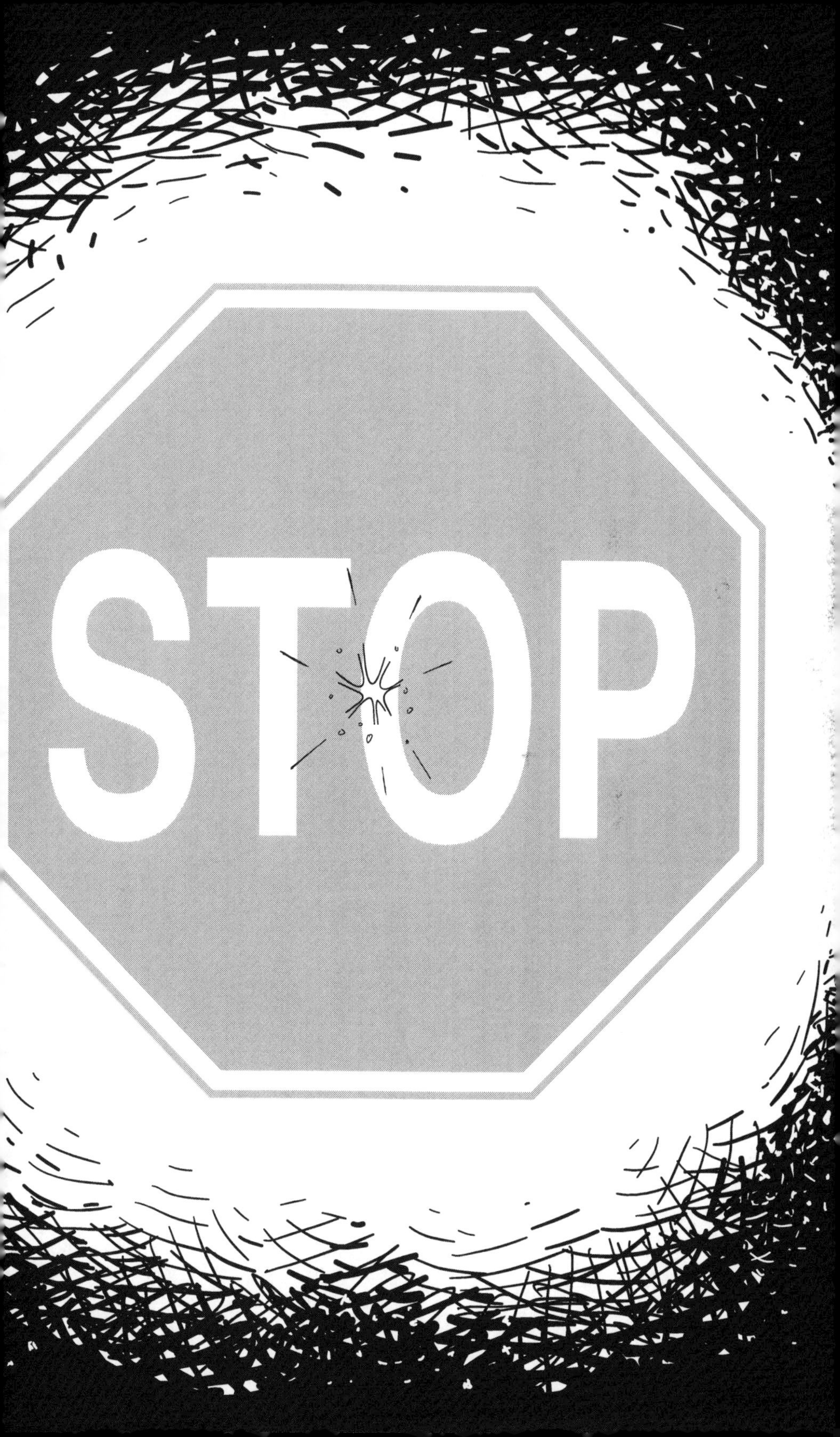
STOP

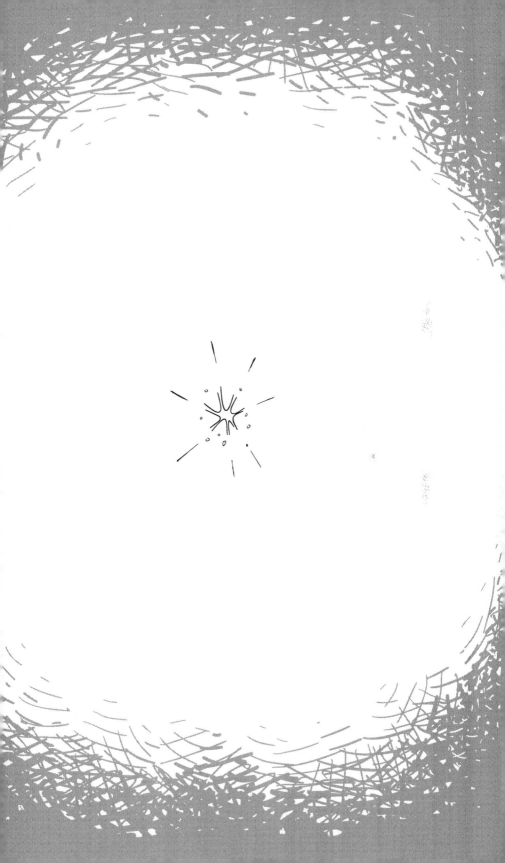

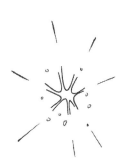

So...

... here you are.

"Now"...

(... and if you'd like to just *enjoy it* awhile,
feel free. Take all the time you like.)

Notice how "this Now" is *different* from the Now you experienced when you began reading?

Notice, too, that in order to think about it, your mind has to come back in and create that past moment for you to "look" at. The reason is simple:

It isn't happening "Now".

You've just popped back out of the present and into the past once again in order to compare the two.

That's fine as long as you are *choosing* to do it. It's only when our thoughts run away with us or become compulsive and we get "triggered" by them that it becomes a problem.

That leads us to the *next* piece of new territory:

Practice *NOW*...

       ... ***before*** you need it!

In order for this tool to be effective you need to practice it over and over again *every day* **before** you find yourself in a tunnel.

Remember that you are creating a new *habit* – a habit that will override the old lifelong habit of allowing your mind and thoughts to run away with you into a fight/flight survival tunnel when something triggers you.

Oh, and by the way, be *patient* with your
mind as you practice. Until you teach
it how to be still it will continue to do
what it does best: *think thoughts.*

That's all it knows how to do. Remember,
it's only trying to *help.*

In time it will learn that there are times to *think*...

... and there are times to *be still*.

Speaking of being still and practicing, remember there's no time like Now, *especially* before you actually *need* it, so...

... before your mind has a chance to wander off chasing those "thought rabits" again, let's practice your new technique one more time.

But *this time*, actually **do it** instead of just reading the words and *thinking* about it...

Allow yourself to take a nice *deep* breath once again. This time, notice any place in your body where the breath might seem to get "stuck" as you *inhale deeply...*

As you exhale, remember that this deep breath is your body's signal that *everything is going to be just fine* so let the breath go along with any tension, any stress, any thoughts of daily life.

As you take an even *deeper* breath now,
breathe right into any place where the
breath might have "hung up" before.

Draw that breath *all the way in*
right up through your body and up
into your head... higher *still*...

... and just let it go completely along
with any remaining tension, any
stress or thoughts at all...

... *ahhhhhhh...*

Now, again, without asking how or why, focus all of your attention on the very *center* of who you really are.

Something in you just knows where that is without *thinking* about it so just **do** it. Focus your attention on where you know the core of your true self is as you *breathe deeply*

into that place, *now...*

… and with a single act of will, as you *exhale quickly*, silently say to yourself the word…

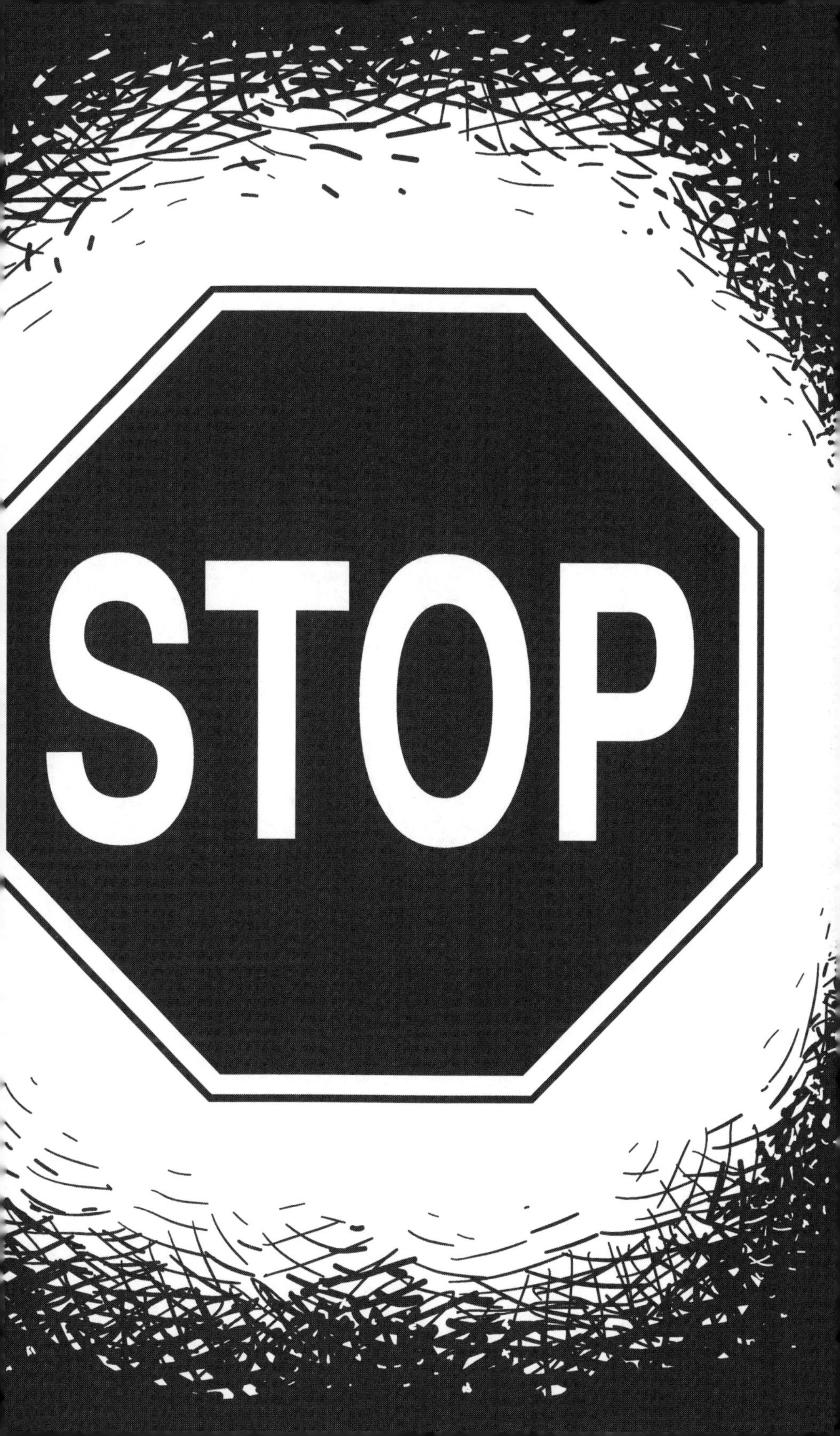
STOP

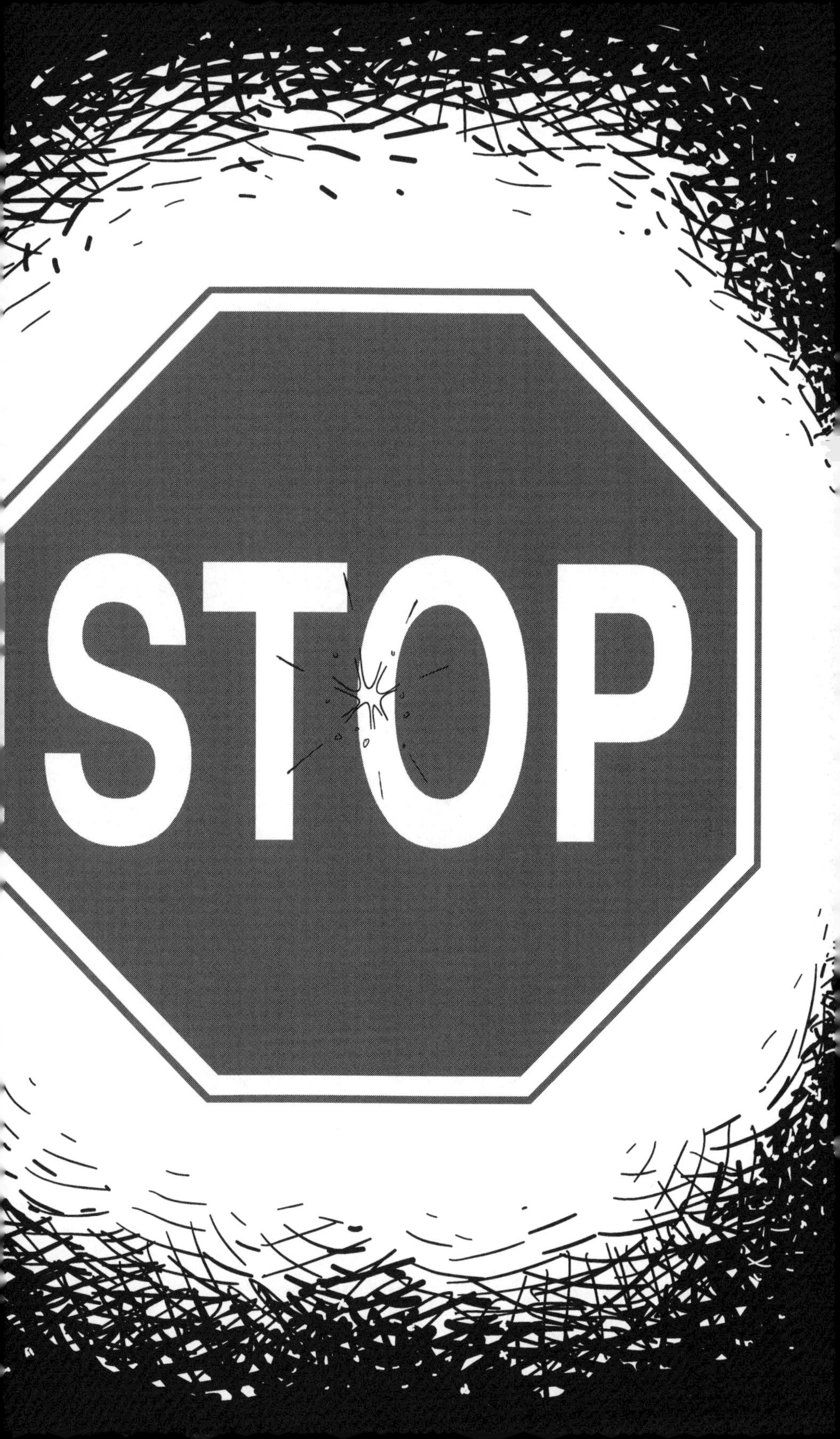
STOP

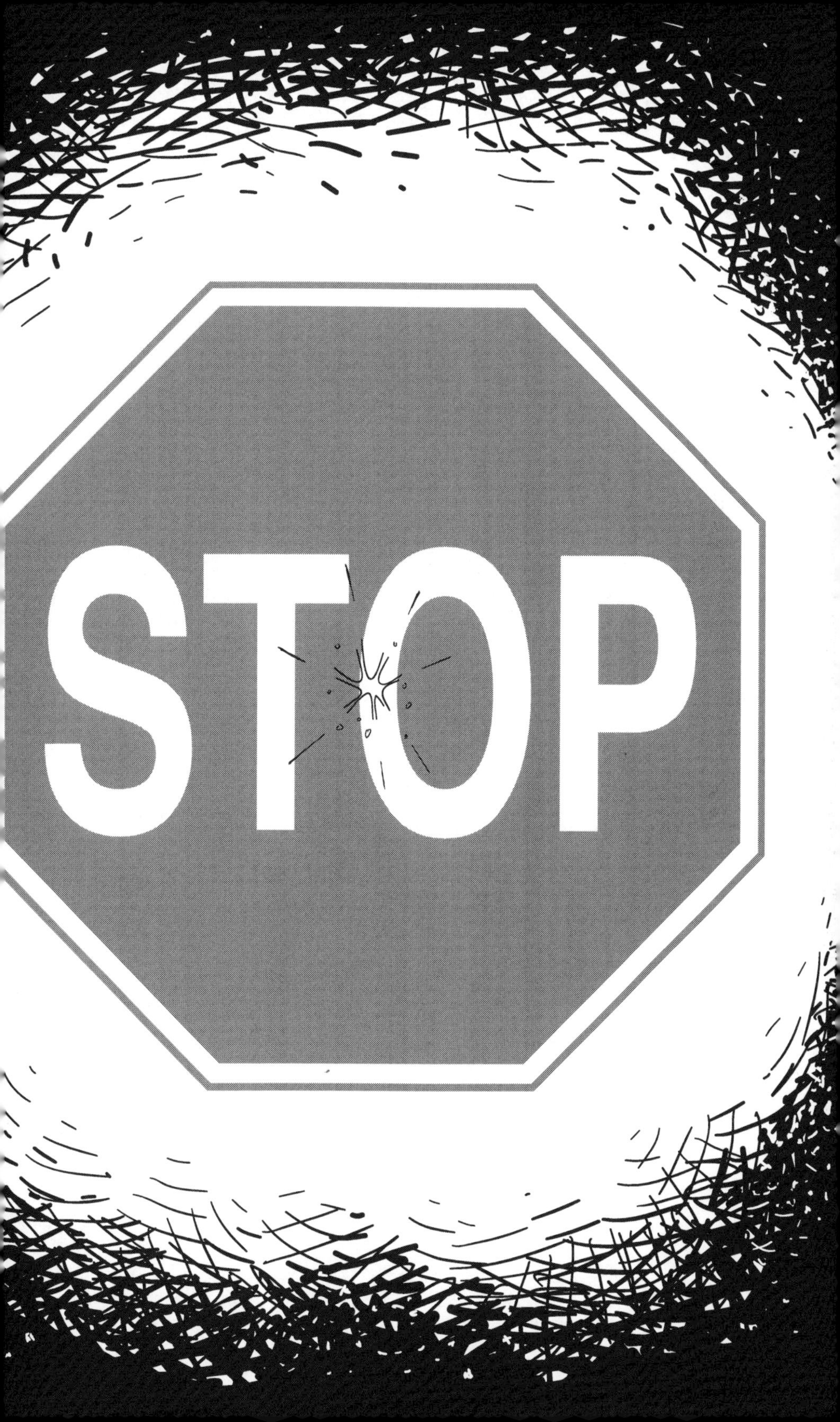
STOP

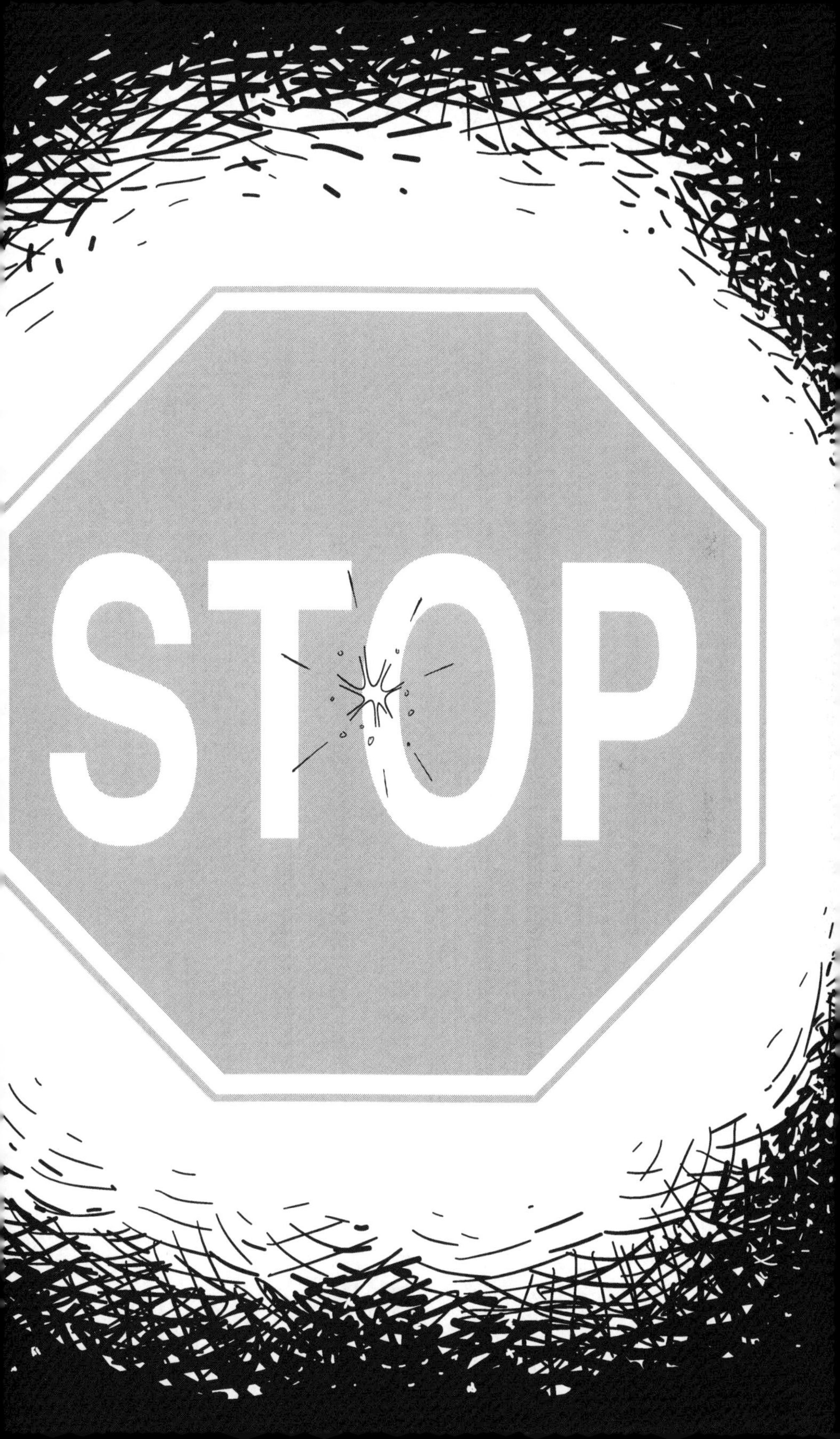
STOP

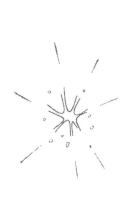

So... here you are. *Now...*

Ahhhhhh... it's getting easier already.

And each time you come back, each
time you repeat this simple technique you
will find yourself a little more calm, more
still, more relaxed and more able to deal
with whatever life presents.

The more you practice, the better you will become at quieting your mind and body when you find yourself triggered.

Practice *often!* You can't do it too much and it only takes a moment.

I promised that this was a book about the *"How"* of Now rather than the "What" or "Why" of Now. My intention is to help you *experience* Now rather than *think* or *talk* about it.

To that end, instead of talking about it anymore I'm including the following section of frequently asked questions from countless clients who have used and benefited from this tool.

Perhaps you have or will have some of the same questions. I hope the answers will be helpful as you learn to master your state of mind and body.

Remember, it isn't *complicated* at all. In fact, nothing could be *simpler*. All it takes is focused intention and a bit of practice. Don't forget, you're always only a few breaths and a *"STOP!"* away from "Now".

Enjoy yourself!

There is absolutely nothing "wrong" with thinking about the past *or* the future. In fact, it's one of the many things that allow human beings to accomplish so much.

It's only when such thoughts become compulsive, *trigger* us and send us into a fight/flight tunnel that we need to stop for a moment By doing so we rediscover our true "selves" and get on with living our lives at our very best.

By stopping the internal noise and chatter from time to time we become calm, relaxed and we regain vital perspective. What better way to learn from the past, anticipate the future and have a healthy, happy and rewarding *present*?

In the end, though, all we ever *really* have is Now, this moment. By living it to the fullest we ensure a rich and fulfilling "past" *and* "future".

There are as many definitions and descriptions for the term "meditation" as there are people. For some, it is a technique of focused thought. For others, it is a simple state of quiet introspection. For still others, it is a kind of mysterious and other-worldly practice from a culture other than their own.

This technique is the simplest and most effective way I know of to temporarily *stop* the almost constant and sometimes destructive *runaway* activity of the mind. The results of such temprary cessation of mental "noise" include increased sense of well-being, enhanced capacity to learn, stress reduction, improved problem-solving, job performance and better health.

The original intention of most forms of "meditation" was the achievement of a still mind. To that extent, this technique is "like meditation".

You're not doing *anything* "wrong".
You were able to make it stop for a
few seconds. Congratulations!
That is a terrific first step. Now
it's time to practice again and again
throughout the day *before* you
actually "need" it.

Remember that each time you practice,
you are creating a new pattern, a
new habit of dealing with the
stresses and challenges of daily life.
It will take some time and a bit
of practice. Be *patient* with yourself.
Each time you do this simple technique you increase your capacity to
make it stop a little more.

Before long, you won't be *thinking*
about it at all. It will be second-
nature to you and you will barely
remember a time when you *couldn't*
make it stop.

This technique is not a "magic wand" for making your problems go away. This is a tool to enhance your capacity to *deal with* the challenges and problems of your day-to-day life.

When you are in a fight/flight survival "tunnel", your perception, your problem solving capacity, your very I.Q. is impaired. You are *anything but* your best possible self.

By quickly and effortlessly achieving a state of calm relaxation, you increase your ability to deal with and solve any problem that may arise by being at your very best.

You are absolutely right. Your problems will still be there when you "come back". Don't be surprised, however, if when you come back your problems don't look quite the same as they did when you were in a tunnel.

Some may not even look like "problems" any more at all.

Keep going! Do it again (and again and *again* if necessary) until your mind becomes at least a *bit* more still.

It's important to remember that this technique is "cumulative". That means that each time you do it, especially when you do it several times in a row, the effect accumulates and grows.

It is also important to remember just how "tricky" the mind can be when it's triggered. You can *think* you're taking several slow, deep breaths and then "stopping" when in fact, you are continuing to let your mind run away with you and whatever your current situation happens to be.

Again, this is why it is so important to practice *before* you actually find yourself in the situation in the first place.

Absolutely. Let's consider what a "diet" actually is. For most of us, it is the constant struggle *not* to eat something that is "bad" for us. I don't know too many people who have a problem eating too much *broccoli*.

For most people, eating so-called "junk food" (or too much of anything) is a way of coping with *stress*. It is a way of escaping from stressful situations by stuffing ourselves with things that taste or "feel" good. That escape, by the way, is the "flight" part of "fight/flight". If that is the only option we have to reduce the effects of being in a "tunnel" then the "urge" to eat the wrong things will be almost constant and overwhelming.

Now imagine being able to step out of a fight/flight stress tunnel any time or any place. Imagine even using the very *urge* to eat something bad for you as your signal to "make it stop".

You're on your way to health and fitness by overcoming one urge at a time.

It's always difficult when one person in a relationship seems to exert most of the effort to "get along". Having said that, let's look at some possibilities.

First, most of the triggers that occur within a relationship tend to be based upon one negative emotion: *fear*. Fear of abandonment, fear of rejection, fear of loss of some kind – most of the issues that arise in relationships can be traced to one form of fear or another.

Second, one way of coping with fear is to attempt to *control* people and situations. While this is not a book about relationships, imagine one where the emotion of fear simply doesn't ever stand in the way of lovingly hearing or expressing who and what each person is and feels. Imagine being able to let go of things that aren't that important and only arise when one is triggered. *STOP*, now. Imagine being able to be *present*, to love someone for who they *are* and choose to either live with them or not *without fear*.

In a word: *Yes!*

Any great sports figure will tell you, "Don't *think* too much!" On the court, the field, the course or in the ring it is vital to be *present* in the moment to be at your best. Of two players with equal skill, a player who is calm, relaxed and "loose" will almost always out-perform one who is stressed, triggered and tight.

The capacity to learn anything from a good jump-shot to multiplication is measurably impaired by stress. Lack of focus caused by the mind racing from "disastrous" past to "catastro-phised" future almost guarantees a negative learning experience.

Learning to quiet the mind so that it can focus on the task at hand rather than dwell on "mistakes" or what "might happen" can make all the difference in the world. It also makes things a lot more *fun!*

One of the best things about this technique is that it is so simple and it only takes a moment or two.

Here's a little secret for those who *think* they don't have time to still their minds. Next time you go to the bathroom (yes, I did say the *bathroom!*) use that alone time to take a few slow, deep breaths and "make it stop". You might be surprised at just how different the world can look after your own private two minute "mini-vacation".

As you get better and better at making it stop, you will also find yourself getting better at finding those little opportunities here-and-there throughout the day to do it even more.

Be patient and you just may discover that you have more "magic minutes" during the day than you ever dreamed possible.

Afterword

I will never forget the first time I watched a client transform by becoming utterly still and present. Since then, I have looked into the eyes of "Now" countless times. Each time I have seen the radiant and limitless possibility of the human *being* and was left awestruck and humbled. I have also had to watch as some faded back into old habits and patterns, limiting beliefs and negative emotions.

There is little in today's modern culture that teaches or cultivates a truly still mind. That can make it difficult for most of us to know what to do with this gift, this *present,* once we discover it. This book is merely a starting point – a first step in what I hope will be a journey of becoming all that we can be.

By making this simple technique a habit, a daily *practice,* we can begin to make a still mind part of our daily lives. In time, that still mind will inform every decision, every interaction, everything we think, feel, say and do. Nothing could be simpler. It requires only moments and very little effort. The only requirement is the *will* to *do* it, not to *think* about it, not to *intend* to do it later but to **do** it... *Now.*

There will be many more books to come – simple little offerings of things to try and gifts to open – all of which will build upon this bedrock of stillness and presence. For now, just breathe... make it STOP... and be well.

Shhhhh...

About the Author

Jim George spent over 30 years in the film and television animation industry and was fortunate enough to work with such luminaries as Norman Lear and Dr. Seuss (Ted Geisel).

He has a thriving hypnotherapy practice in Venice, California where he lives and works with his wife Peggy.

43024284R00138

Made in the USA
Middletown, DE
28 April 2017